FEEDING THE FEAR OF THE EARTH

FEEDING THE FEAR
OF THE EARTH

Poems by

Patrick Lawler

Many Mountains Moving Press

Denver, Colorado

2006

Many Mountains Moving Press
www.mmminc.org

Library of Congress Cataloging-in-Publication Data
Lawler, Patrick J.
Feeding the Fear of the Earth/Patrick J. Lawler with a preface by Susan
Terris.—1st ed.
ISBN 1-886976-18-X

Manufactured in the United States of America.

Designed by Jeffrey Ethan Lee.
Cover art: b/w photo by Courtney Frisse, 1993, of "Dora and Lucy," by
Gail Scott White, who named these seven-foot-tall sculptures after two
women that Freud analyzed.
Copy editing by Jan Carroll.
The text is set in Garamond with title page text in Caslon540.

ACKNOWLEDGMENTS
These poems (including some variants) appeared in the following: "Black
Elk and Petra Kelly Visit Love Canal" in *Green Fuse*, "Ed McMahon Meets
Marcel Duchamp through the Mails" in *Shade*, "Alan Shepard Floating in the
Heavens Sees Christa McAuliffe Falling through the Sky" in *Talking River
Review*, "Ptolemy Follows His Map to Sojourner Truth" in *Red Brick Review*,
"Humphrey Bogart Plays Yorick after Falling in Love with Sylvia Plath" in
Ohio Poetry Review, "Those Who Died in the Triangle Shirtwaist Company Fire
Find Themselves Working in Hamlet, North Carolina" in *Many Mountains
Moving*, "Ana Mendieta and Chico Mendes Fall Down in the Waters at
Sandoz" in *Controlled Burn*, "Virginia Woolf Touches the Cerebellum of
Albert Einstein" in *Boston Literary Review*, "Blake Watches Mr. Milton's Angels
Burning in Madame Curie's Hair" in *Shade*, "Madame Blavatsky Meets
Magritte Sleeping in a Window" in *Yellow Silk*, "Martha Graham Dances in
Stravinsky's Burning House" in *Oxford Magazine*, "St. Dymphna, Carrying Her
Crying Heart, Comes to Lacan who Carries His Own" in *Cream City Review*,
"Ynestra King and John Muir Breathe the Air in Bhopal" in *Birmingham
Poetry*, "Marx Dancing with History Meets Marquez Dancing with Time" in
Americas Review, "Mickey Mantle sees Isabel Allende Holding the Head of
Hermann Hesse as he Dreams of Mother Eve" in *Many Mountains Moving*,
"Mengele Invites Pavlov to Look through the Eyes of the Dead" in *Sycamore
Review*, "Egaz Moniz Meets Marshall McLuhan" in *Defined Providence*, "A
Dream of Langston Hughes Blossoms in the Head of Carl Jung" in *American
Letters & Commentary*, "A Doctor from Tuskegee" in *Rockhurst Review*, "Murray
Bookchin and Susan Griffin Buy a Home in Love Canal" in *Synaesthetic*, "Aldo
Leopold Thinking Like a Mountain Meets Andre Collard Living Like One"
in *Sycamore Review*, "Anne Sexton and A. Gordon Pym Stay Afloat in Madame
Tussaud's Wax Museum" in *Georgia State University Review*.

DEDICATION

For my friends and colleagues, poets and family—with gratitude and love. For all those who have shared, inspired, and encouraged. To my students: without you there would be no need to write.

jendawnseanphyllismallOryamyrichmelaniemarlenechaunlloyd
juliebrendadudleymargaretemanueldan
poojalorettaalbertkazanaligregphilutumnbrandiwendymilescesar
christosarielleeuniceshreyasroannewellingtonpamheidikristen
stephanlauraannajeffshelbyaprilleia
jasoncolleenjenniferorlandomelissapeterevelynwaynemarilyndaniellelogan
anjaleebrittanyaudreybarryjillscottryangretchenstephen
shaneandreakristinericjusinshandorsujarhoneyvette
sharonmarkkenelenraycharliemike
taratomjeffnicoLecaramarikalindakirstenkatiepablosusankim
maryjanineseandavidrainaalexandrajaVierpaul
marciachrisjEsusricardomaryellenbasildylanlauraandrewmattsuzanne
brixkendallsandrageorgeruthgenanthonyterryamanda
shannonkathydollygordonneilpatbenettedawnelle
betsytimcaroldavidbrendon
gaildawnchristinesarahjoejeffbevbillchuckdanjimpattyrickadaM
TiffanyjayheatherkellymeghanwhitneyfrandOn
evancourtneyemilybrantmeredithrosalynmarissadanaeriklisastacyjenijerry
jeanamberjaunitasharijedlandonaaronsaratracykimberlytheresa
brucerobinannemariealiciavinnycandysammarianne
garyannhenrydottiedaveroseanne
laurenbrianrobynstanchrisginakenjodimorgan
tanithnickmeaghanjuliatonylennyjudyned
georgiacelietompaulkathymaureenjimbonnielindsayray
juliegordOnnealkarelsuebrianhollybilly
rachelchellseajuliekathynneyyegary
jocelynmariojoshjamescandacejanemikeeuniceallisonmatt
grahamkevinjoanbrendonsherijacobtinajohn
denisejennyclarajoejennifersylviabrucezacharyshalalucy
janetnic

Special thanks and deepest appreciation to Sandra, Shannon,
Chris, Michael, Gail, Billy, Jim,
Susan, Naomi, Jeff, Erik, Jeffery B,
Linda, George, and David.
Your enthusiastic support, your suggestions, your generosity,
your love and friendship
are responsible for the shape of this book.

Especially for my biological, emotional, and spiritual parents:
Anna and Earl
Santina and Frank
Barbara

Thanks for the time and support given me through a SUNY ESF sabbatical, a Saltonstall grant, two NYFA fellowships, and an NEA fellowship.

Preface

by Susan Terris

Patrick Lawler's *Feeding the Fear of the Earth* is an outrageously original collection of poetry. The premise of the book is that well-known figures of historical and/or contemporary interest intersect in surprising and significant ways. Therefore, in the course of this wonderful book: Emily Dickinson takes Pablo Neruda for a boat ride down the Hudson as they listen to the music of Tchaikovsky, and Humphrey Bogart plays Yorick after falling in love with Sylvia Plath. Just reading the table of contents of Lawler's book is an adventure in itself.

This is a book that can be read from the first poem to the last in sequence starting at "(black elk and petra kelly visit love canal)" and ending with "Anne Sexton and A. Gordon Pym Stay Afloat in Madame Tussaud's Wax Museum." Or, after glancing through the table of contents, you can turn immediately to read about such diverse figures as Mengele, Langston Hughes, Tonto, Ed McMahon, Virginia Woolf, or the ever-fascinating and still-dead Jim Morrison.

Lawler's poems are electric, eclectic, ironic, intellectual, and funny all at the same time. He's making statements about science, politics, religion, history, and race but all with a deft touch. He's never didactic or heavy handed. By profession, Lawler is a professor of writing and literature in an Environmental Studies program, and his subject matter is always concerned with what man is doing to foul this environment versus those who would make it flourish. The tension of this juxtaposition is what drives this collection.

Lawler is at home with the odd, the surreal, but it is not only the images of these poems that will move—even haunt—a reader, but his charged use of language. When "Blake Watches Mr. Milton's Angels Burning in Madame Curie's Hair," the poem concludes:

A woman watches Dresden under a night of shooting stars.
The next time you open your door, a woman
Will be standing there, burning like a ruby.

I want you to believe this. She will be burning,
Burning, burning. And you will see something else.

At the same time, however, beyond Lawler's verbal ability
to invoke the image within the image, there is a persistent
directness and accessibility to his language. In his poem about
Mickey Mantle, Herman Hesse, and Isabelle Allende, therefore:

> When I'm in Mexico
> Mickey Mantle
> is dying of cancer.
> Once I burned
> his baseball cards
> in a shoebox—
> a symbolic gesture
> of leaving.

In addition to the charged, eccentric tone of Lawler's
language and the contrasting plain-spoken voice, he also soars
into lyric in a way that is magical and compelling.

What I really want to say is: read this book. *Feeding the Fear
of the Earth* is fresh and challenging. It was a privilege to judge
a competition containing a manuscript of such power and
vision. Lawler is a poet of skill and conviction. His work will
amaze you. It will frighten yet elate you. It will make you look
at the world in which you live in an entirely new way.

CONTENTS

ONE

§   §   §

TWO

§ § §

THREE

§   §   §

ONE

(black elk and petra kelly visit love canal)

§§

It happened
in the time
of moonsuits
entering
basements.
It was a time
of shovels and
claustrophobic
boots.
It was a time
when everyone
was trying to
fuck something
or someone or
someone else's
catastrophic
aftermath.
It was a time
when time was
ground up into
history. It was
a time when we
named our
countries after
poisons. It was
a time of tiny
empty houses
and abscessed
streetlamps.
In a town made
of candelilla
wax, abstract
streetlamps
burned in the
empty streets.

Dante Saying *Arrivederci* to Hell Sees
Mary Wollstonecraft Riding a Dolphin

Life's too big a place to be only one person.

Excuse me, but I wanted to be able to send packages to the
        dead—
maybe letters—descriptions of what it's like without them.

In ecstasy, I feel my eyes collapsing.
I am a moral sensualist.
There's the crime scene,
but I'm used to the contradictions.

I am disappearing a little at a time:
I wake up and my concept of self is gone.
A month later, my navel.

The first world is fire.
And after that, nothing is possible,
except water.

I'm in a detective novel and I'm all the suspects and all the victims.

When I walk around in my body, I feel I am trespassing.
It contains something that is other than me, foreign and forever,
something that marvels in the more.

A biopsy has been performed on my heart.
I live in a loophole.
I am my own body double.

My eye is replacing me,
replenishing me,
ravishing me.

The real problem is double vision:
    heaven & hell
    male & female
    life & death
    self & other
    body & mind
    word & world
    culture & nature

In the flickerings of identity, I'm going home to find parts
    of my body.

Following someone who looks just like me
except a different gender,
the detective is relentless.

The real problem has to do with the way the eye works.
But, I guess, I already said that.

Someone who looks a lot like me yearns for an alchemical touch—
something to say we are real and all that is real is changing.

Someone else says
he is me,
and I don't think
he's lying.

Ed McMahaon Meets Marcel Duchamp through the Mails

I just received a letter from Ed McMahon
saying I won $10,000,000. Not bad.

I once knew a woman and we sent holes
to each other through the mail.
White sheets of paper with circles cut into them.
That's when I fell in love with the great mystery of the mail.

Ed McMahon looks happy.
But it also appears as if he has a dirty face.
I wouldn't want someone handing me $10,000,000
if he had a dirty face.

They found a hundred pounds of undelivered mail
burning under a Chicago viaduct.
There is always the danger
that whatever we say ends up on fire.

> When I was in sixth grade
> I was in the slow class
> with a number of older students
> who'd failed quite a few times.
> I tried to say a mistake had been made,
> but no one listened.

I sat behind a girl named Barbara,
and she sat across from this older boy
named Richard.
He would take this thing out of his pants
and lay it on his leg.
I had never seen anything like it.
It seemed to have a life of its own.
At first, Barbara didn't want to look,

but then he'd sing a song for her.
Or maybe the song was for this thing
that moved in his lap.
A few years later he was serving
a sentence for stealing mail
from the Post Office.
I don't know if these two things are connected.

I feel sorry for Ed McMahon.
It is as if he never had a life.
If I won the $10,000.000,
I would invite him over
to sit on the couch and chat.

I go to the mailbox as if it were a tabernacle,
as if this great mysterious river of things were coming toward us
and this is where it stopped.

Ed McMahon asks, "Will I be awarding *you*
$10,000,000? It could all depend
on what you do right now." I feel
the pressure. What happens
if I don't do anything?

And then I'd like you to explain this:
I got this thing in the mail that said UFOs
are from volcanoes. According to this, UFOs are really
volcanic material that travels thousands of miles.

What are they trying to do:
take away our hope?

A woman and I once sent holes through the mail.
All we wanted was for each other to fill them.
And now I write a letter to Barbara. Or want to.

It begins: Barbara, I'm suspicious
about this $10,000,000 thing.

It appears that Ed is lying or at least
                                  exaggerating.

I try to say a mistake has been made
but no one listens.

I hear they found a mail truck in NYC
with this burning mail in the back.
All the bills, all the faces of Ed McMahon,
all the catalogues of the 10,000,000 things
that keep us sad. And the words—
maybe 10,000,000 words—flickering and flashing.
These fire words. These flying words.
They fill these holes inside us
with something that feels like hope.

Alan Shepard Floating in the Heavens Sees Christa McAuliffe Falling through the Sky

When I'm pretending to be something else,
      My daughter is bewildered.
She understands how vigilant we must be
If we are to stay who we are.
"You're really my daddy. Right?"
I'm not always certain what I should answer.

She misses some of the things
That have fallen out of the sky:
Pieces of a spacecraft,   detritus, debris.
Other things she takes for granted:
An angel with a wing   on fire,
Fat flakes of snow, bell sounds in a burnt-out church.
A black wreath dropped in the dumb sea.

              Someone I know gave birth
The day the astronauts fell out of the sky.
She can't really get their falling out of her head.

I tell my daughter some of this—
How birth sometimes looks like something else.
Still, she touches my face when I'm pretending
To be a gleaming stone or a vanished magician
Or a fanatical horse. Every day she gets more accustomed
To how inadequate the sky is for holding things
                in place.

One day I'm a   very   old astronaut,
And my daughter understands completely.
Hunched in my spacesuit, I've lived for years
On this lumpy planet—half shuffling, half floating.
I see this woman who has these people
Falling in her head. We touch our hands
Where they've been   burnt.

Puffed out in my bloated white suit,
I'm a bulimic ballerina slowly rotating in space.
    I circle the rusty satellites
That haven't worked for centuries;
Probes that have gone   crazy,
Sputtering and chugging along, no clue

As to why they exist; space stations
Like tin cathedrals long abandoned.
And I see this woman who has these windows
Floating in her head. I don't know what to believe anymore.
I tell my daughter   I am really me.
She says she is not certain what she should answer.

Those Who Died in the Triangle Shirtwaist Company Fire Find Themselves Working in Hamlet, North Carolina

The machines are the first to know something is wrong.

At the loading docks, the trucks are hollowed out.
The men count their parts before ascending,
Move to the inside of the shop.

Those who've died in factory fires wait for us.
Women hunch over the sacred, hollow place
Of a chicken or stand in front
Of rivers of cloth vanishing into the machine.

I work in a wire mill; the wire spins
Out of the machines, delicate elk
In copper forests. The wire turns on its thousand
Spools—meridians for an interior
Globe, the intricate webbing of a thin ship.

Those who've died in factory fires
Always walk among us. The union people sign
Them up; the foreman demands their quota of work.
Every one of them carries the smell
Of burnt flesh, but we get used to it.

In the tinning rooms, the wire leaps,
Silvery, equatorial.
There is an icy spider in the breast.
During breaks, men gnaw at *Midnight*, glow.

Women make themselves seductive,
Polish the dark back into their hands.

The burn victims mull over us.
When a hand comes back, it is a screaming thing.
They walk toward the bosses. The smell of burning
Hair makes the brain shrivel.

Breaks in the wire. The pupils
Dilate like drops of hot solder.

I mic a spool of wire in the smoke, holding it
Like the skull of Yorick. The finest wire as thin
As baby hair is groomed
For a government contract. My hands detect
The brain of the spool. Messages about the next
Village to be burned sizzle through it.

Humphrey Bogart Plays Yorick after Falling in Love with Sylvia Plath

I needed all the names for death:
Blue-eyed traveler and everything else.
Philip V of Spain believed he was already dead,
And so he refused to eat or drink.
This is instinctively true of the dead,
Being economical by nature.
Maybe this perchance to dream business

Holds the best back. But I have discovered
The dead do nothing for themselves.
They don't even duck.
Still, I needed all the names for death:
Perfection, winter, solitude, sleep, fountain,
Leaking boat, splendid afternoon. All the names:
Philip V, blue-eyed traveler, and everything else.

Right now, the sky is like broken berries.
Right now, ice is everywhere. Winter hangs its thin
Bones in the thorn trees. Life is like someone
Visiting the body. Death will be the same—
Something without a name,
Something swallowed, something from outside
Saying, "I am here. I am here."

Ptolemy Follows His Map to Sojourner Truth

I unfold the map that was given me

by my father. I find none of the places

remain. Countries get lost in the creases.

Names have been changed. Cities have moved.

I never know whether to believe in nothing

or believe in everything. The body snaps,

then seals shut. Certain countries have vanished

from my father's face the same way the world

went out for brief moments around Berkeley

when he shut his eyes. My father

had dreams older than sleep,

had a guide who was already gone.

I follow the stuff of the skies, the tears

in the map, the rip like a road. To believe

in everything: the phoney borders, the illogical

routes, the darkness that is part of the system

of stars, the system of stars that is part

of the darkness. To believe in nothing

I have traveled a long way, the length

of my voice. I have found myself

in a foreign country whose skin is like bread.

I stand on the scorched edge of a city

map— boulevards like boxes, rectangles of road.

I wander in spiraling word maps of the Pueblo

while my mother unrolls her map of Neptune,

bumpy and blue. "Here is a place."

How monks must unwrap

the pearly light of the world each morning

before breakfast. Even for them certain words

give up. I read a map

of windroses and light, a map of the mouth,

a map of the pulse. I stand on the edge

of a map of rain. I follow the fire

on a map of wax. I believe in nothing.

I believe in everything. I believe in nothing.

The rivers on the map begin to move.

§ § §

(ana mendieta and chico mendez fall down in the waters at sandoz)

§§§

It happened
in the time
when water
carried familiar
bodies with alien
faces, when fish
floated in translucent
poison, when red
fishermen's hats
lazily sunk.
It happened
in the time
of the crystal
evening, of sea-glass
and algae, of darkness
entering the eyes
of fish. It was
a time when we
were so close
to invisibility
we could feel it.
It was a time
of grogginess,
of the ponderous
obliteration. It
happened in the time
when we were
healthy. It happened
in the time
of our choking.
It was a time when
we were so
complete we could
watch our
unsuspecting deaths
float past us.

Tonto has a Dream (Deganawidah Removes a Mask from a Living Tree)

I was watching Tonto and the Masked Man.
Tonto always seemed quiet, but that made him
appear wiser—more restrained, as if an inexplicable past
were being filtered through him. I'm sure the director
thought of that. It heightened the tension. Quite frankly,
the Masked Man seemed a little dumb,
never sticking around for thank yous. And what the hell
did he mean by Hi Ho Silver? I never understood

where he came from.

You see, I couldn't have been at the Trail of Tears,
at Rattlesnake Springs where the soldiers gathered 13,000
Cherokee in the Removal Policy. I wasn't there
when they were forced 800 miles from their home.
I wasn't there at the end when a quarter of them were dead.

I couldn't have been with Jackson when he had his soldiers
count the dead by cutting off the noses of the Creeks.

I was watching TV in the 1950s. I was watching Tonto,
and I never understood where the Masked Man came from.
I mean, why did he have to wear a mask if he was good and all?
It was almost as if he were trying to hide something.

I wasn't there when they took Geronimo away
for twenty-five years as a prisoner of war.
I wasn't even near the Navajo after they were marched
to Bosque Redondo where they were starved to death.
I wasn't at the winter camps on the Washataw River
when Custer came to slaughter.

I was watching Tonto, concerned that for the 1950s

he seemed a little inappropriate.   I know he had a sense
that he had come from somewhere, but now maybe his life
was better because of the Masked Man. You got
that impression. At least, some people did.

And even if I lived back then, I wouldn't have believed
that stuff about savages. I mean, if they taught it,
if important people said it, like politicians and generals
and priests, I guess it would have some
influence, but not to the point of being paid $50 for Indian scalps,
not to the point of condoning genocide,
not to the point of turning belief into action, or if it did
turn belief into action at least not to the point
where it would be too destructive—I mean, irrevocably
        destructive.

You see, I couldn't have been at the Sand Creek Massacre
where the soldiers slaughtered 200 children, women, and elders—
Black Kettle's people. I didn't burn the camp.
I didn't cut off the skulls and send them to the Smithsonian
in little boxes for someone to study.

I wasn't at Wounded Knee when Big Foot offered the surrender
of his 350 starving Lakota people. I wasn't there
when they were slaughtered, left dead on the cracked snow.

I couldn't have been. It was the 1950s, for Crissake.
I was seeing everything for the first time. I was watching
white and black TV. How could I have been anywhere?

And even if I were, I wouldn't have participated.
Even if they said I had to shoot, I would have only
shot once or twice. What could that have done, really?
And, anyway, I was watching Tonto and the Masked Man.
Even though I could never figure out that whole thing
about the mask and why he felt compelled to wear it.

19

Virginia Woolf Touches the Cerebrum of Albert Einstein

At 25 mph I am ready to burst into a hummingbird

or an auto

at 60 mph I am all the green

barracuda water I am breathing

doing 70 I turn into a cheetah

or a Tibetan swift

faster than endless lusciousness

I am sound

before I am light

faster than wax I turn into color

a little faster and I am a Matisse

I am Hiroshima when it is fiercely falling

I am the flesh

with its insurrectionary song

at certain speeds I am an anarchist

or the electricity inside a brain

at certain speeds I leave

myself

behind

Motion (Zeno) Puzzles through Spring (Carson)

          (the white) (tail deer never) (step out
from behind)
             (blue spruce)
     (in this system of snow)
(snow cannot fall into itself)
                  (so it won't)
      (have to become itself
   over and over)

                                  (look

           to a species)

              (made entirely)   (of flowing)
      (life
moves) (in its multi-lectical fashion)
       (not in these pretty) (intellectual
  arias) (which prepare us
for imagining) (the silence of the planet)
                (look to a species
                made
                entirely
                of imagining)

                                        (whatever language) (this is)
                    (a language) (we can never leave)
                    (the shadows are not
                                        tucked neatly
                              under the trees) (sparrows)
(sputter) (in and out) (of the sunlight)
                                        (in and)

                    (out)
                    (of the shadows
                              that fall
                                        from every
word)   (this is)

(the turtle
                                        under its constant) (stone sky)
                    (does not have to teeter) (to its
                                        appointments) (anything
can happen) (but it won't) (a heron
          on the unsteady
                                        angle)
(of its leg) (stands forever) (in the cool
                    water
                         that flows) (daringly past)
                    (the
                    only
                         survivor)

                    (stone)
          (a constant companion)

Petula Clark Sings to Rodney King on the Edge of a Burning City

1.

      "What you

think you

               see isn't

      always

         what you see."

2.

I carry my video camera everywhere I go.
I'm focusing in on you
Because I know something will happen to you.
Something terrible will happen to you.

I carry my video camera everywhere I go
Because I have amnesia.
Because the part of me that carries
The past—whether it resides in the pouches of my head
Or the sack of my heart—has been removed from me.
Because I have this thorn in my throat.
Because I am tired of the punctures in my heart.

3.

I carry my video camera everywhere I go.
I have seen George Bush presiding over a smoldering city.
Only his head fits into my camera.
His white head like a beach ball
Left out in the sun all summer. Like a hive
Of albino bees. He was in full control.

Ladies and gentlemen, the president was in full control.

4.
I carry my video camera wherever I go.
I have seen Petula Clark singing in a burning city.
Petula Clark whose first name sounds like the sexual
Parts of a flower, whose last name sounds like a candy.
Only her voice fits in my camera.

[To the tune of "Downtown"]
Dadadahh dadahh dadadahh.   Downtown.
[Everyone.]
Dadadahh dadahh dadadahh.   Downtown.

Linger on the sidewalks and the neon lights are pretty
Look at all the cops and addicts—everything is shitty
Look at Danny Quayle dancing in a burning city

How can you dance? The lights are so much brighter there
You can forget all your troubles, forget all your cares

And go downtown—That's where the homeless are
Downtown—Where the city burns like a star
Downtown—That's where the pain is bright
Downtown—Hope you get laid tonight
Downtown—That's where the neons know
Downtown—Hope you enjoyed the show

Downtown
Downtown Downtown

5.
Downtown L.A. Downtown Detroit. Downtown Birmingham.
I carry my video camera wherever I go.
Downtown New York. Downtown here.

I have seen Rosa Parks flying over a burning city.
I have seen her bus full of dreamers wobbling in the night sky.
Stars burning above her: the street burning below.

A fire in a pet shop: a monkey screaming
In a cage. A Radio Shack crackles below her like bones being
    broken
In a swan's neck. I say, "Get outta here, Rosa. Your people
Are dying." And Rosa with more passion, more wisdom,
More courage than I continues. Her eyes expand
Seeing all my video camera misses. She tells me what she sees.

Petula Clark teetering on the edge
Of a banged up city. Her downtown dying.
She sees images of Martin and Malcolm rising from
The cash registers when she knows they're seated
In her bus. She sees the fire lighting up
The written voices—the graffiti alive like cats
Screeching on the walls.

I yell up to her,
"If something isn't done, Rosa...."
And she says, "Put down your video camera,
You fool.
How can you see anything with that contraption
In front of your head."

I'm sorry, Rosa. I carry my video camera
Everywhere I go because I can't stand things
Touching my eyes. I carry my video camera
Everywhere I go because something terrible
Will happen to us. Something terrible will happen
To us. Rosa, I can't see you anymore,

But I know you're up there giving birth
To the next century. Flying black lady
Guided by the fire in the sky and the fire in the city.
Guided by the golden fire in your mouth.

Everyone.

Jim Morrison Dressed as Nietzsche Meets St. Francis Dressed as a Bird

When looking for God, you must always start with windows.
Take them apart. Do it in winter
So you can quietly arrange the glass bodies
In the comfortable snow. Allow the light to shine through
The red yarn of St. Anthony's intestines.
St. Sebastian, pierced and dreamy,
With a face like a teen idol. St. Lucy carrying her eyes
On a platter. Next the cold marble, the cumbersome statues.
Dance them out to the edge of the snow banks.

And after you have set up the scaffolding and pulleys,
You should lower the chubby bell and roll it
Like a clanging barrel down the steps. Next, carry the Madonna
Delicately onto the grass. It will be spring by now.
Be careful not to chip her aqua breasts or look too closely
At her lip. Finally, lug the big crucifix onto the back
Of a truck. Adjust it so the blue eyes of Christ look out over

The lawn on this spectacle of angels and statues and colored glass.
The beeswax candles. Try not to think of the heat; summer
Is burning behind you by now. Try not to say anything
About how truth, if it is the truth, cannot be believed.
The sun caught in the bottle of St. Lucy's eye,
Sparkles with new wonder. As the truck pulls away through
The dust, Christ clutches that berry of blood in his hands.

Blake Watches Mr. Milton's Angels Burning in Madame Curie's Hair

The burning lady of Toronto burns in her building.
Her dress ablaze, she spreads to the hallway

Of her apartment, knocking on doors where some
Reluctantly answer. Smelling the sizzle of her ribbons,
A man opens his door a slit. "Spring must be here,"

He says to his wife. The burning lady burns;
Her lips spark. A woman looks through her peephole,

The burning lady blazing on the other side. "Ah,
The lucrative light of the noon. Isn't everything amazing?"
Another opens his door to the theory of fire. Still

Another to the beginning of time. The ashes
Of her housecoat singe a trail in the rug. A fat man

Watches the heart of a dancer bursting. Her shoes
Turn into smoke. Another sees an angel with a flaming
Wing or sees a sinner about to repent. He can't

Tell looking through the monocle on his door.
While the burning lady stands in her combustible shoes,

A woman watches Dresden under a night of shooting stars.
The next time you open your door, a woman
Will be standing there, burning like a ruby.

I want you to believe this. She will be burning,
Burning, burning. And you will see something else.

TWO

(edward abbey and kathini maloba build a fire at three mile island)

§§§

*It happened
in the time
when all
psychotics
were named
Ralph. It
happened in the
time of the
egg, when we
kept patching
the shell so
nothing would
come out.
It happened
in the time
when our bones
were turning
to glass. It
happened in
the time of all
the dead Elvises.
It was a time
when we were
astonished
by the sexuality
of fire, by the
ossification of
everything else.
It was a time
when we forgot
the meaning
of words, and
still they found us
sleeping.*

Madame Blavatsky Sees Magritte Sleeping in a Window

Correcters of Accidents to Procure Sleep.
       Against fearful dreams, madness, etc.
Nymphea. Violets. Saffron. A woman is thinking

Of walnut trees where owls want to sleep.
They, in turn, are thinking of trillium and silk.

Try rose water and vinegar with a little woman's milk,
And nutmeg grated upon a rose cake
       Applied to both temples.

       Behind it all a woman is dreaming
About the way we are composed.

She is standing on a subtle shore,
       Watching the water
Until there is only a soft rag-gray.

Everyone I love is sleeping in a strange house
       They call sleep—their glands

Like pouches filled with shaken snow.
Experiment with rose vinegar and valium.
       We are going backwards now.

Everything we once feared we must fear again.
Backwards. Windows turn back into sand,

       Sand into boulders, and boulders
Into mountains we can see through.
And everything we once loved we must

       Love again. Sleepers curl

And soften—are made small—a woman

So small she can enter her own vagina.
        The white dreamless owls grow plump.
Lovers in every imaginable combination—

Skin glistening, as if they had spent the night
In a forest—touch before they are swallowed.

Margaret Mead Discovers William Burroughs

Because I live
in the earth
in a house
of stone,
my eyes have
no color.
The sky is
a different story.
The rivers
no one named
turned to
granite. The radio
trickles through

this rock room.
My grandmother's
womb is made
of stone.
My mother's womb
is made
of stories.
My mother says:
Whatever you
bury in the earth
you bury
in my head.
My grandmother

all day weaves
the rope that
will take her
downward,
moving her from
    one world
to another.

My mother teaches
me to be water.
One river is

named Sleep
and it solemnly
enters the room.
With my head
among the roots,
my grandmother
hands me one
end of the rope
and warns me
not to follow.

Freud with a Picture of Teiresias Finds Dora with a Picture of Cassandra

When I wake, glass is all around me.
Millefiori   glass.   Venetian glass. Glass
with thin vein-like cracks. Glass like
the breath of an anorexic.
          Glass like the brains
of deep-sea fish. Glass like language.
Glass like belief. Glass filling the room.

Glass like echoes. Glass like the language
of aboriginal people. Glass from the mothering
caves of memory. Glass like swollen objects
that have been misplaced in dreams:
Birthmarks and terrariums.

Glass like the uterus of a saint. Glass

like the sewn language of memory. Glass ready
to break into a mosaic. Glass like a body of someone
touched. Glass like an indelible language.

Glass like the memory the body has
of places that have been touched.

Glass filled with twisted light. Glass so fragile
it breaks when I think. Glass that cuts into flesh.
Glass that grows more dangerous
with every step. Glass that sees everything
with its shattered eyes. Glass like a fantastic
plant with fruit that will make us transparent.

Martha Graham Dances as Stravinsky's Music Plays inside a Burning House

I grew up in a house   that had once burnt
       down before I was born. Sometimes we
Could still hear
        the brisk-blue linoleum bubbling
        under our feet.

    The past wouldn't stop.

The furniture glue
Would run down the legs of the chairs.
The wooden bowl of fruit would fill
         with an orange   glow.

      An inexplicable
      flash
And the stairs would   collapse.   A flame
      would creep
      up the stem   of a wallpaper rose.

    Lightbulbs
    snapped and burst
    Into tiny red cracks.

                And my sister
Sat at her piano playing Stravinsky. When finished,
A fire rose out of the palms of her hands,
Her fingers blackening like ribbons. My mother
Lectured about smoke, how to crawl on all fours.
My father   desperately knotted sheets
                       together, testing how much weight
                       they would hold, trying

                to rescue us

                       from something that had happened long ago.

At night   the house just couldn't be dark.
        A chair would spark; a raincoat
        would melt   into a bright yellow pool.
Sometimes a book crackled and curled
                       and
                       went black
                       in our hands.

Light
Could happen   anywhere,
        a blessing breaking over us, a fever, a glow.

St. Dymphna, Carrying Her Crying Heart, Comes to Lacan, Who Carries His Own

Heavier when naked, I'm
Too deep to imagine.
My breasts

Hang like bees' nests in a barn.
If I become

Barbed wire,
No one will touch me.
If the father says

The word "beautiful,"
I'll never get out.

I approach permanence with rage,
Come to fear with inspiration. I
Fear the pills as they are slipped

Into my system,
Eclipse and scatter.

The father is in the mind
Digging a hole.
He can't get out,

Can't keep his hands out
Of the dreams of his daughter.

Winter tumbles
Toward me
Like a thrown knife;

It stiffens in the heart.
I fold my naked legs

Like an old man's spectacles.
A woman of elegance again,
I order more walls.

I stand up with my bones
And I holler.

Hélène Cixous Meets Georgia O'Keefe Painting a Picture of the Madonna's Heart Filling Up with Snow

A weaving goes on in the mill
Of her being. In the winter there will
Be a birth. The blue fuzz of light

    In a farmhouse window. The snow
    Wishes it were a woman. The sounds:
The spinnet of the inner life, the
Distance unraveling until space and

Time are one. In dreams, I wipe
    And rewipe the frosted window panes.

    I weave my philosophical system out of
    Snow. Make the world familiar; make

The world strange. The barns are full
Of wondering cows. The child, among
Cut crystal, among the bluish silver
Of ice, peers into the carats of her
    Mother's eyes. I listen. I wonder.

    I listen for the winter and then

For the thaw, for the cracks in the ice
    And the cracks in the weather. I listen

    For the clock being shut up inside.

Behind us, the past
Has totally disappeared,

I want to know what the light learns
When it touches the child for the first time.

Marx Dancing with History Meets Marquez Dancing with Time

I'm listening to the flesh radio, and it says: After they burn
       the villages, they burn the books. It asks: Is anyone
       listening?

I'm listening to the mouth radio, and it says: We need
       Khlebnikov's "star language." It says: When we open
       our mouths, the night sky falls out.

I'm listening to the fire radio, and it says: Marx is watching
       a light burn in Macondo. It says: Conquerers
       are drinking the galaxies. It asks: Who can remember
       the victims?

I'm listening to the moon radio, and it says: La lah. La lah.

I'm listening to the word radio, and it says: People are
       forgetting the meaning of words. Each word says,
       "Walk through me."

I'm listening to the gland radio, and it says: We live in a land
       of violet crimes. It says: A word is stirring on the edge
       of the universe. It says: After they burn the sky,
       they burn the windows.

I'm listening to the dream radio, and it says: This just in...

I'm listening to the weather radio, and it says: Tomorrow
       everything will be brown. It says: The next day
       everything will be intellectual. It says: The day after
       everything will suffer in blue.

I'm listening to the Nagasaki radio, and it says: Forget
       everything you ever knew.

I'm listening to the world radio, and it says: Subvert
the apparatus of cognitive control. Subvert the
apparatus of cognitive control. Subvert the apparatus
of cognitive control.

I'm listening to the chromosome radio, and it says: The radio
is thinking through you. It says: The radio is
thinking for you.

I'm listening to the light radio, and it says: The light
meanders slowly through the brain of a cat. It says:
Every morning light remembers and then gradually
forgets.

I'm listening to the womb radio, and it says: The mother
grows around the child.

I'm listening to the meat radio, and it says: Red is
throbbing outside the window. It says: We need
to stop giving birth to mammals.

I'm listening to the brain radio, and it says: America.
And it says: America died in 1900 something. It says:
After they burn the people, they burn the dreams.

I'm listening to the star radio, and it says: You cannot.
It says: You cannot burn the memories of the burning.

§   §   §

(ynestra king and john muir breathe the air in bhopal)

§§

It happened
in the time
when the breath
of animals was
taken—in a time
when people
didn't want
to watch throats
anymore.
It happened in
the time of
our mother's
murderers.
It was a time
when we couldn't
see. It was
a time when
we couldn't see.
It was a time
when all angels
and saints and
shamans and
gurus had vanished.
It happened
in a time when
we couldn't
get out of our
brains quickly
enough. It was
a time of empty
shoes and
dysfunctional bees.
A time when we hated
to watch our finger

puncturing what
came out of our
children's mouths.

Christopher Smart Brings Van Gogh's Ear, Like a Flower, to Anne Sexton

1.
Glass speaks and it says, "Glass." Peach says something,
horizon says something else. Though we can't see him, the
woman's retarded albino son daily performs feats of astounding
devotion—

> while the man
> sings himself
> to the moon.

"This is the Crystal Hotel on the day the police allow us to
dream." The dead father leaves messages on the tape recorder.
The woman has a child's painting: two sailboats slip over blue,
and a big heavy sun is dug out of the sky. She carries this
picture as if it were a window. The man's mother has turned
herself into a bee with eyes as big as plates.

> The woman is
>
> listening
>
> to her corpuscles
>
> talk to each other.

At the windows all the roads are taken away. The man looks
at the snow as if it were coming from inside him. The mirror
speaks and doesn't remember any names. The man works on
the project he calls "Meaning." When children who have lost
their fathers are asked to paint pictures, invariably they have
bright yellow windows full of sunlight.

> Sunlight, you see,
> is the color
> of dead fathers.

2.

The woman is a figure skater with her feet on fire. It is as if she lives one glide ahead of her own catastrophe. Through the concordance of their experience, the man and the woman go looking for the word *luminous*. The woman takes pictures of her face with his hands. She carries her passion as if it were a window. The world is seduced from its silence;

the world is caught

shimmering

in its own

specific flame.

Meanwhile, another man and another woman in another world touch entirely, setting everything into a state of constant vibration with their hands.

They are astonished
daily

to learn they live in separate bodies.

Dorothy Arzner Looks in the Lens of Her Camera and Sees Caroline Herschel's Comets Falling through Adrienne Rich's Eyes

Inside the camera everything looks squished.

Devoured by the   glass lens,   I'm tiny.

I am sitting in an empty theater
waiting for a movie to come on.
My waiting   is the movie.

It's just like Andy Warhol—except it's tedious.

I'm watching previews of my dreams
and feel my body   fill with sight.

> *When my clothes*
> *catch fire,*
> *I take that*
> *as a sign.*

I am making a movie of this woman's mouth.
   She is a book
of light   I can never close.

And then the director asks:
Who do you think you are?

Someone is playing John Wayne and he is mad.
Someone is playing Marilyn Monroe and she is sad.
Etc. Etc.

I am sitting in front of an empty silver window.
The only thing I have left is this fear of asphyxiation.

I hear:
      Cut.
       Cut.

And I know exactly what it means.

I take up again the issue of   the   real
and enter a poem by Adrienne Rich.
It gets scary at this point.

I have melted   into the camera.
Hollywood is killing my identity, but I feel happier this way.

    Here the movie changes direction.

The telescope swallows.

Motorcycles like hornets in a coffee can.
Crash scenes. Bullets.   Flying.

The movie changes direction.   Everything is soft.
   In the last scene, I am living with a woman's mouth.
The aquarium where my heart grows.

Cut.

Cut.
Cut.
I look at the world around me and know exactly what it means.

Egaz Moniz Meets Marshall McLuhan

We bring in the first head full of storm clouds
And lightning. We bring in the second head
Full of cactus gardens and smoke. We bring
In the third head that sounds like a crumbling
Stream when you put your ear to it. A long river
Of gurneys winds in back of us. You must understand.
Never enough time to do what we have to. We bore
A hole in the skull and disconnect the diencephalon.
We take out the desires like pieces of misshapen
Crystal. Sometimes a butterfly will emerge
From the drilled hole and sputter around for a brief time.
You can see the urgency. Or a deficient egg will roll
Out on the table. Or a fat bee, full after drinking
The dreams, will flatten itself on our scalpels.
To speed up the process we take picks through the eye
Socket to eviscerate brain tissue. Surely, you must believe
It sounds worse than it is. The eye drips a diamond. The issue:
To be more efficient. We need to enter
The brain on a daily basis. We need to relax you
So you'll have relief from your desires, escape
From your memories. We have to do something
With the thousand years of light inside your head.

Donald Trump Holds the Mirror for Narcissus

Today I've decided I will buy everything I've ever seen.

I'll sit in front of the blue light specials and let the light fall on

        my neck as if I were a saint.

I'll buy an aquarium and have things wave at me from behind

        the   glass.

I'll buy all the books by people who have been dead at least

        100   years so I won't have to read them.

I'll purchase the delicious, the dangerous, an anchorperson

        with a   perpetual smile.

And later I'll buy a car with fancy wheels, with a mirror for an

        exterior.

   I'll dream of carpeted miles.

I'll buy ceramic dalmatians and yellow daisy lawn fans

                     to spin lazily and applaud.

I'll buy a country.   I'll buy a pretty eye   to swim behind.

          (I can't wait to buy another me.)

I'll sit in the shopping malls and dream of empty stores, all the

        products

piled in luscious mounds around the fountains.

I'll see myself in the windows of the shops, the sweet mall music

slipping

around me.

Mickey Mantle Sees Isabel Allende Holding the Head of Hermann Hesse as he Dreams of Mother Eve

•

When I'm in Mexico,
Mickey Mantle
is dying of cancer.
Once I burned
his baseball cards
in a shoebox—
a symbolic gesture
of leaving.

•

The seas are rough around Cancun.
Black flags on all the beaches.

•

Everyday I go looking for a   *milagro*,
miniature figures: body parts, inner
organs, animals. They are offered
to a saint to commemorate
a miracle or to ask the saint's intercession.

•

How do you say:

"I am an American,

and I am prepared

to buy everything you have"?

●

I'm going to go swimming with the dolphins.
I'm going to go diving into the strange—as if words
were a species, as if desire were a species, as if pain
                    were a species.

                    ●

            I dream about
        parachutists
                in bright colored jump suits
                falling through the sky.

●

This is the week when we celebrate
dropping the bomb on Hiroshima.
        The usual parades.
Shadow floats. Balloons filled with tears.
Helium carried by men and women
                with melted hands.

                    ●

            On the way to Tulum,
            I dive into a cenote,
            a hole into an underground
            river, a lavish mouth,
            a fantastic eye filled
            with holy water and forgiveness.

            ●

        Everyday I look for a   *milagro,*
        little medals made of tin or silver or gold—
        wax or wood or bone.
        If you have a headache,
        the *milagro* will be in the shape of a head.

If your heart is hurt,
it will be in the shape of a heart.
You pin them on a saint
and everything is made better.

●

How do you say:
"I am an
American,
and I will sell you
everything
you will never
need"?

●

I am afraid I will not find
the appropriate   *milagro*.

●

It is 8:15 a.m. August 6, 1945.
A six-year-old boy waits
on the platform of the Hiroshima Station.
He waits for a train that vanishes as it arrives.

●

I dream about parachutists—
1,000s of them in brilliant yellows,
whites, and oranges dropping out of the
        sky
in the field next to the house
I grew up in as a child.
They are on a secret mission.

•

A woman rubs my hair and says it will cost
a certain amount of pesos for the room,
a certain amount of pesos for her body.
        She offers me the cenote.
The delicious waters of her skin.

        •

A Mexican friend and his wife feed me
in a bungalow of sticks and tar paper.
La casa de mis suenos. They are proud.
She is pregnant.   I am American.

•

I needed someone else other than my father
to be my father. Mickey Mantle
stumbles around the bases.
                The ball will never land.

        •

I look for a *milagro* for Mickey Mantle—
something in the shape of lungs or wings.

    •

Fifty years ago we set the sky on fire.
        Robert Lewis, the copilot
of the Enola Gay,   writes in his
                journal,
"My God, what have we done?"

                •

                I look for
                milagros
                with melted

                hands.

•

It is 1961 and I am dying.
My eyes don't need me any longer.
It is 1995 and the parachutists
come and announce
I've been dead a long time.

•

I want   to give   my Mexican friend
a *milagro*   the size   of a fetus.

•

The sea's shoulders are collapsing
under the pinned moon.
One-hundred-fifty-thousand people
come out of the sea waving black flags.

•

How do you say:
"I am an
American"?

•

In Hiroshima they float
brightly colored umbrellas and lanterns
on Hiroshima's seven rivers
to remember the dead, to remember those
who drowned trying to cool
their burning bodies.

•

Tonight, there will be an aluminum moon
pinned to the sky.
I won't go swimming with the dolphins.
It's 1995,   and America
will put Mickey Mantle in a shoebox.

THREE

(vandena shiva and henry david thoreau touch the black waters of valdez)

§§§

*It happened that
it did not
happen in the
time of the first
mother or in
the time of
sacred snow.
It happened
in man-time
when we needed
to destroy
that it happened.
It happened in
mall-time
when we needed
to destroy
time. This was
a time when
silence and
contradiction
were jewels—
a time of
stickiness.
This was a
time when we
could feel
the TV crawling
across the carpet.
It was a time
of ethereal static—
a time when we had
to buy something.
It was a time
when shore*

birds touched
each other before
they died so
they would
know what they
were joining.

Mengele Invites Pavlov to Look through the Eyes of the Dead

Before he took them into the experimental rose gardens
and had them shot, Mengele called in the dozen dwarfs for
measurements. He knew after you snap off the head of an
animal everything gets easier. The finest Jewish tailors worked
all night by candles, cut and stitched the tails and the gowns.
When the dwarfs returned to his

chamber, the males carried their top hats like thimbles. The
lady at the piano played Schubert and Puccini. He knew that
if you pulled the spinal cord out you could watch a body
flop around. He could tell you exactly how many seconds it
would take. The dwarfs waltzed about the room in graceful
maneuvers. They drank vodka from tall glasses, did

tailspins on the freshly waxed floor. He knew you could force
feed poisons until those experimented upon would die a death
called *writhing death*. He knew about rhesus monkeys, squirrel
monkeys, twisting cats. The inevitable small talk: the merits of
Wagner. "It must be beautiful this time of the year in Berlin."
The men held onto their women, cradled them

like expensive violins. He knew that if you remove the vocal
cords from the throat you can hear yourself think above the
chatter and the screams. The dwarfs had reached a kind of
perfection where tomorrow isn't possible. He knew he could
insert an electrode grid to the skull to make a tiny finger twitch,
to make a mouth wobble as if it were praying, to make

his dwarfs embrace like stone dolls. The abstract ashes fell
through the night sky. In the name of science and perfection,
the abstract ashes fell through the night sky. The dwarfs could
hear the music on the other side of the door. Woozy with
Schubert, the dwarfs, like fat drunken bees, tumbled into the
garden. Mengele knew he could make the dead dance.

Aung San Suu Kyi Quenches the Thirst of Leonard Peltier

a river
is put
in the cell
of the prisoner

every day
it is a source
of torture

every day
the prisoner
must watch
its silkiness
its glistening

every day
the prisoner must
be rescued
from it

the sumptuous
reminder
of all
that is behind
the river

and all
that is

waiting
in front
of the
river

one day
desperate the prisoner
swallows
the river
opening the
mouth

the prisoner
flows
out
into
the
streets
past the nodding

guards
who've
died of thirst

A Dream of Langston Hughes Finds Itself in the Head of Carl Jung

On one wall the wallpaper hangs in strips like the petals
Of a black flower. I am in my uncle's house after a terrible fire.

The inside is exposed: beams, studs, wires. Charred things.
     No windows.
My brother is pulling down insulation.

He has already gutted most of the house. An elaborate
     chandelier
Of wood and metal and ropes and hurricane lamps

Hangs from the second floor ceiling like something you
Would find on a clipper ship if clipper ships had electricity.

It is the brain of the house—dazzling and dangerous.
Worried, I say I should check the foundation,

But I don't. My brother climbs the chandelier. He looks
Desperate. Currents run through him

As the lights dim and sizzle. A black woman
In a maid's outfit appears. She is lovely.

She writes poetry but she doesn't tell me. She asks
If I want to see her room. It is blue—a deep

Eye-like blue, as if we had walked to the center of a pupil.
Little twinkly lights on the walls. A window. Wallpaper

Like a wave. A canopied bed. Everything is a thick liquid
Blue. She says, "I thought I could live here, but I can't.

The smell of smoke is in everything." When I look

Outside the window, I feel the house shift like a stack

Of toy blocks. It begins to crack and tumble. As we fall, I can see
The world maneuvering in slow motion through space. I ask if we

Can kiss. She understands but says no. Still, as we hold onto
            each other,
This blue room comes free from the burnt house.

We're falling. And we land so softly we hear nothing break.
When we emerge from the room, I am the same color

As the woman who is no longer dressed as a maid. She wears
            a dress
Of parrots and sun. When we emerge from the room, children

Are waiting for us. I dream I write
this all down because it seems urgent.   My brother is a child.

A Doctor from Tuskegee

After all, it was a long time ago.
It was different then. Working in Tuskegee.
Ripe and swollen. The sun always hanging in the sky
like the bell part of a stethoscope.
All the cotton made the place seem muffled.
I guess you know we studied black sharecroppers
with syphilis. We never treated them.
For forty years we just studied the spread of the disease.
A scientific experiment.
We told them they had bad blood
which wasn't far from the truth.
We promised them money for their burials
which wasn't far from the truth.
I'd come in with my lab coat, my stethoscope, my clipboard.
I'd have the nurse take their blood pressure, their vital signs.
You should have seen them.
"Doc, I can't get the smell of my own death
out of the pillow." And there was always that Macon
County sun moving across the sky
as if someone were shoving it across our chests.
People don't understand. Sure we could have saved them.
But what kind of experiment would that have been?
Some people make a big deal out of the fact they were all black.
Let me tell you that was almost by accident.
About a hundred died. I can look through the reports
if that number is important.
I don't know why I have to explain this to you.
I've said you have nothing to worry about.
Come back every couple of weeks. We'll do urine
samples, blood tests, some X-rays.
For now sit up on the examination table.
Yeah, I know it looks like butcher paper. Funny.
You have absolutely nothing to worry about.

Emily Dickinson Listening to Tchaikovsky Takes Pablo Neruda on a Boat Ride Down the Hudson

I get a phone call from a friend
who tells me his mother is dying
in a hospice, in Albany.

My friend who is a psychiatrist
tells me he watched her put food on a spoon.
The simplicity and grace struck him.
He told his mother how beautiful it was
watching her put food on a spoon.
How this gesture seemed to capture the essence of life.
And she asked him why.
He said it was because it seemed
to illuminate the preciousness of each moment.
And she said, "I felt the same way when I got my microwave."

I've had this sense of something missing in my life—
an essential ingredient, a meaningfulness.
I've decided I need a sidekick.
An Eddie Murphy or a Starsky or a Sundance.
Maybe B. J. Hunnicutt or Thelma, as in, Louise.
Someone to share my adventures.
Someone who's there even when I don't want them around.

Once I went to the wake of someone I didn't know.
It was by accident. I thought someone else
had died, but it was really just a person
with the same name. I was looking for a familiar
face, someone to share my grief, but I didn't
recognize anyone. When I went up to the casket,
I said, "Holy shit, this isn't the guy.
This isn't the guy at all."

And I thought: how durable life is.
I mean, one minute you're there.

And the next minute you're there.
The only difference is that, without anyone noticing,
someone with your name is gone.

If I had a choice, there would be a lot
of people with my name.

Recently I've been having this dream about playing basketball.
My father and I are playing. Whoever wins
will come back to life. I'm playing very hard.
I'm sweaty, out of breath, aching. My lungs
ready to pop. I am behind.

At one time Jung was Freud's sidekick.
I imagine them on a boat fishing,
talking about their mothers, their fathers, their fears,
catching nothing in the scintillating sunlight.

My friend fears that his mother's death
will take away his childhood.

I am still eating the last blueberry pie
my mother will cook. She tells me her bones
are being devoured from the inside.
One day they'll snap out from under her
like glass pencils. She's shocked that she's old
and points to the pills she has taken.
It's hot, she says. The skin of each berry is punctured.
The ooze of dark juice. I can't wash the stain
from the Tupperware dish that seems to be bleeding.

I want to go somewhere and tell death
my mother no longer exists. She moved, she disappeared,
she relocated, she got a fucking U-haul
and headed off into eternity without ever passing through you.

While I had his attention,
I'd feel silly, but I'd ask him how my father is doing—

whether he's still practicing his jump shot.

I hope when I die someone will come to my wake
who doesn't belong there.
Someone who'll just stop in—looking.

My friend tells me he wheeled his mother
to the solarium to watch the fireworks over the Hudson.
It was the Fourth of July. She was very happy.
She watched the darkness with these piñatas of fire
bursting around her. The light like cracks
in a cathedral window. Chalices pouring out blossoms.
This endless hatching of one miracle after another.
It would be impossible to recover from such beauty.

I want to tell my friend there will be plenty
of sweaty nights ahead—playing basketball,
playing hard just to keep the dead from winning.

It is like a full-time job.

I want to tell my mother I know she is growing
old and afraid, and I am right behind her.
I want to tell both of them
the world is ridiculously beautiful.

I want to put an ad
in the newspaper: Sidekick wanted.
Someone who will be content to spend
long hours on a boat
watching light fall out of the sky.

I want to take my mother to the Hudson to see this fire
cracking up the sky. This chrysalis made
of stained glass. This piñata of scars
and light. Sometimes I am sad and sometimes I crack
with joy. It is getting to be impossible
to tell the difference.

§ § §

(lois gibbs and john burroughs watch stars crushed over chernobyl)

§§§

It happened
in the time
when god lived
in a nuclear
reactor. It
happened in
the time when
our thyroids
were glowing
with science and
picks. It
happened in a
time when we put
a great light
in the earth.
In a time of desire.
In a time of
philosophical wax.
In a time when
rain could kill
your child
if she ate it.
It happened
in a time when
we feared to look
at the body
in the body
we loved the most,
afraid we would
find our own
deaths. It
happened in a
time when we
were promised
nothing
would happen.

Mahmud Darwish Meets the Hibakusha
Shuffling Across a Soundless Bridge

1.

On the night we burn the sky over Baghdad
    my daughter asks, "What is the longest
    war?"

2.

    The Napoleonic Wars.
The War of 1812.
The Civil War still wet on school desks.
    You can still eat dinner
    in front of Vietnam.
You can still watch B29s
diving through the skies over Germany.

3.

Hermocratus, a general for Syracuse,
    was condemned to exile
for having ordered his troops to treat
the invading Athenian armies with moderation.
That is why Hermocratus is not here.

4.

Because the imagination has already given it shape,
    our absence is always with us.
We are living in the world after the bomb dropped.
Nothing makes a sound beneath our feet.

5.

I see General Sherman on *Nightline*.

The Hundred Years War is being covered by CNN.
The Boxer Rebellion comes with commercials
for Nike.

6.

One of the rules: You are only allowed to question
if you are losing. Believe me: I'm losing.

7.

I wonder where Hermocratus went.
        Some Greek isle
working in an all-night Seven Eleven
fearful of the next customer—
fearful that the next customer will look like us?

8.

What happened to the musicality, the ring one hears
in the word *Crimean?* What happened
        to the War of the Roses—genial, poetic—
something to write on crosses in the English rain?

9.

The *hibakusha,* the survivors of the nuclear bomb
we dropped on Japan, walk through life
        as if they were in
        a '50s science fiction movie.
No one knows who they are until
someone tells them it is all right to scream.

10.

I receive the message that nothing is wrong.
And after that, I receive the message that nothing is wrong.

11.

We weave white flags in the air; we wear black
        gloves to the office.
We do only enough to ensure our immortality.
Nothing more.

12.

This week,
the child with no skin
        does not appear on the cover of *People* magazine.
So we will buy it.
So my daughter can look at it and want to be all
the happy people who are dwelling inside it.

13.

In the warm sunshine on the other side
        of this planet, Hermocratus is fearful.
Moderation. Moderation. He is no hero.

14.

On the way to sleep, we step over the bodies
        fallen in our house.
For the first time, I cover my daughter's eyes.
        She is preparing me to see.

Murray Bookchin and Susan Griffin Buy a House in Love Canal

I got this plan.

I want to live in a place
where in the morning
you can leave your three-bedroom
ranch and look over
to your neighbor leaving
his three-bedroom ranch.
There's something consoling about that.
I want to live in a place
where people say,
"How are you feeling?"
and really mean it.

In Love Canal the sky walks
over the tense trees. In Love Canal
the autumn sky looks like meat.

Some people think it's crazy
to sell homes in Love Canal.
Some people think I'm crazy,
but that's not always a bad thing.

This guy named Harvey
is trying to sell
me a house in Love Canal.
He says it is the safest place in America—
the testing, the monitoring wells,
the habitability reports.
And I look at the plywood on the windows,
and it makes me warm.
I feel this humming deep inside me.

It's important to have good
neighbors, especially if you live on top
of a toxic waste dump.
And I tell Harvey I want him to be
my neighbor. Harvey's eyeballs
        begin to melt.

Let me tell you about this:
I get sick of all the fear.

Benzene. Dioxin. PCB.
Trichlorobenzene.

It's hard to get worked up about things
you can't see. Oh sure, there's
a town in Mexico where babies are born
without any brains.
But we live in America,
a place to meditate on
the remarkable aftermath of civilization.

And there is something holy about this place
called Love Canal—
it is as if all the roads leading to it
had been devoured by birds.

Harvey tells me the story about Love Canal:
The man named Love, his search for Utopia,
Hooker Chemical, the hysterical housewives
(especially Lois Gibbs), the hysterical housewives
who couldn't stop thinking about their wombs.
But Harvey says we must be reasonable.
And I know it's guys like Harvey who
got America   where it is today.

Harvey tries to keep the air
from falling all at once into his body.

I want to buy a home at Love Canal.
I want to live inside the American Dream.
I want a wife out of a lipstick ad
with hair like cotton candy.
I want to drool over her.
I want to sit in the sunny kitchen
with the pink appliances and the microwave
like a coffin for one of those kids
who do their starving on TV for everyone to see.

So how are you supposed to determine
the habitability of a place?
I understand Harvey's point.
I mean what are we supposed to do—
live on acres and acres of glass
so we can see everything below us:
the shiny mechanical intestines of the earth?
So we can see right straight down
into Dante's House, into the crawling
things inside his brain. So we can see
into the stooped. So we can marvel
at the blue chemicals bouncing
inside the head of Persephone.
So we can stare forever at her mouth
as pink as poison.   Come on.

Harvey says six people still live
in the uninhabitable zone.
I see a mail truck putter
past the boarded up houses.

I tell Harvey I like the idea of having a big fence
around the place they say contains 20,000 tons
of toxic waste. It makes me feel safe.
I tell Harvey I got a plan.
Harvey's head spills out of the collar of his shirt.

You know, I wouldn't mind being named Love.

It's a good name for meeting people in bars.
I bet I'd get noticed.

I once knew a woman who lived at Love Canal—
a neighbor of Lois Gibbs.
She told me how spontaneous fires
used to errupt in her backyard.
Not bad for barbecues.
She talked about her whole family having

bone tumors. But you can't always blame
everything on everyone else.
She said the kids who grew up at Love Canal
have no enamel on their teeth.
But I don't know if that's a bad thing.

You see, I want to live in Love Canal.
I want to live in a place like the place
I grew up in—with the TV always on.
It was pleasant and nice and pleasant.
Then they put a sign outside our house:
           Slow Children.
I didn't think they needed to advertise it.

Back then, we didn't need to know
what was beneath us. Back then, we didn't need
to imagine all the bubbling in the earth.
I mean nothing beyond the sexuality:
the tulip roots, the green fleshiness,
the bright pink buds. I mean,
we didn't go down to the raw and the desolate.
We didn't get through the mud drab layers.
The amber layers. There was much
we couldn't see, and we knew it was better not to.

I say, Harvey, it's you and me.
But listen, I don't want to live where you're selling
the homes, Harvey. No, I want to live

in the uninhabitable zone. I got this plan.
I'll take everything into my backyard.

And Harvey tells me about Lois Gibbs.
How they put her witch black dress in the picture
window of her home and bulldozed it down with glee.
"Nothing but a housewife with a hairdresser's education,"
he says. I imagine the workers delicately fingering
the button holes of the dress, dreaming of the pink
hairspray smells clinging to the fabric.

I got a plan, Harvey. I'll let my basement overflow.
The chemicals will move like plasma through my pipes.
My faucet will be the discharge pipe of the world.
I'll fill vials with Love Canal. I'll sell them
                on the shopping network.

And I'll put my mouth to the faucet
and feel the whole chemical world
filtering through me. Jesus,
I'll be the patron saint of toxic gush.

I can tell Harvey isn't comfortable about something.
He tries to keep himself
from vanishing into a cavity that is opening
up behind his back.

No. No. Listen to this.
I could be the mailman at Love Canal.
In my grayish-blue uniform and with a
certain mailman attitude, I'd deliver all these letters
from all the sweet habitable zones.
And then I'd take away these packages

            filled with the sky of Love Canal.
            Filled with the silvery, tender
            insides of Love Canal.

How much better could life be?

Aldo Leopold Thinking Like a Mountain Meets
Andre Collard Living Like One

for Nicole

We took away their breaths and wondered
Why they wouldn't breathe. We
Shattered their homes, replaced the brains
Of bees with electricity. The chipmunk
Like a rolled up sock; the urgent squirrel;
The male cardinal like a scar.
We wondered why they were afraid.

      Snow child. Winter child.
      What will we feed you?

The next moment never steps into the next moment.
I read the eyes of animals, see how
They turn flesh into light, and light into flesh.
See how they flex. Whole again, unfrozen,

Healed. I feel the liquid lynx
Spilling through my house. Think like a mountain
When they scrape down the trees. Think
Like a gazelle, the sun in the belly.
Think like a rainforest thinking of blossoms
Filling like cruets with rain.

Think like a sea turtle
Opening its slow eyes and the music of everything
Rushing inside. Snow child.

Winter child. The red sun goes down
Into the bloodstream. Nothing is swifter
Than the eye when we look at the deer
Looking at us. Nothing contains so many
Questions. When will we finish
Feeding the fear of the earth to our children?

84

Whole Poems

In Cambodia they have a thriving industry
in wheelchairs and artificial limbs.
Thousands of landmines are hidden
in pockets of earth
throughout the country—Claymores
and Chinese models.

In the '50s my father broke his back—
fell off a ladder while he was welding
at a chemical plant. For years
he had to wear a back brace and fight
a Workman's Compensation case
he barely won.

If you walk in Cambodia, you are in danger.
The antipersonnel detonating devices.
The trip mechanisms. The booby traps.
The Soldier's Manual of Common Tasks says:
"Install the Claymore facing the center
of mass of a kill zone." The fragments spray
and rip and cut. With patient malice,
the mines wait for years,
thinking all the time their meaning
is undermined until finally
they exuberantly burst. The Chinese model
is propelled upward out of the ground
and reaches a level about the height
of a child's face.

With his broken back, my father didn't work
for years while my mother saved
Green Stamps and we lived in a cellar.
Instead of a house, we lived in a stump.
A cave with a flat tar paper roof.
With tiny rectangular windows—too far

above our heads, too small to let in any light.
Green Stamps like moss
grew all over the tables.

The ex-soldiers and farmers and mothers
and school children drag the lower parts
of their bodies like sacks
along the roads to Phnom Penh.

My father's back brace looked like the rib cage
of a prehistoric reptile—like something
you'd find in a Spanish monastery
during the Inquisition.
I didn't want to look at it.

There are two messages here:
whatever stays in the earth is dangerous
and whatever stays in the earth will save us.
And, of course, there's something else.
In a lab in Massachusetts researchers
are growing human ears on the backs of mice.

Scientists grow the tissue by first creating
an ear-like scaffolding of porous,
biodegradable polyester fabric. Human
cartilage cells are placed throughout the form,
which is then implanted on the back of a
hairless mouse. I wonder

what would grow out of my father's back.

I've always been aware I had a certain destiny.
Right now, I'm supposed to be in Cambodia,
making artificial limbs. I'd make elaborate
prosthetic devices. I'd gather gears and grease
and grinding things—levers and wheels.
I'd work with tubing, haywire, parts of a red
bonnet. I'd make limbs from small engines

and balsam and wax. I'd make windmills.
I'd work with putty and glue, with tintype
and spokes, guitar strings, and plastic.

I'd gather kindling and gourds—
the insides of clocks, tassels, colored ribbon.
I'd whittle crutches into ships.
I'd gather things that sparked
when they rubbed together. I'd take out
the thin insides of pens for veins.

What I want is delicate machinery to carry
pain. What I want are carousels
for fingers, music boxes for hands.

I say: Rise. Get up. Please, walk now.

But my father digs his way down into
his house, and my mother dreams of birds,
collecting them in books. And me?

Whole legs grow out the backs of mice.
Whole poems rip out the back of my father.

Anne Sexton and A. Gordon Pym Stay Afloat in Madame Tussaud's Wax Museum

Edison is there.
And Ali and Picasso and Elvis.
There's the Queen of England
in a Las Vegas crown—
the sumptuous flask of Mae West's
body. Fire turns them into fountains.
Their hands, a soft sign language
of surrender, a malleable quote.
Their melting speaks of the luscious
disfigurement of philosophy
and flesh. The ultimate merging
of everything. They know
what they love is what they fear.
This is what heaven looks like:
the terrible screams
of the Many slipping into the One.
Hegelian synthesis gone crazy.
Their faces become spores,
each of them surrounded
by the death of the other.
When it is over, we look into
what was once their mouths—
a bee released from their bellies.
In the real world it is the same.
The wax river. The wax boat.
The wax man who can no longer
shrink from the fire his hand
carries to his throat.

Patrick Lawler's Series of Poetry Books

For twenty-five years Patrick Lawler has been
writing a quartet of poetry books collectively titled
QUINTESSENCE and inspired by the four elements.
Each book is both a part and a whole. University of
Georgia Press published the first in the series: *A Drowning
Man is Never Tall Enough* (1990). The second book, *reading
a burning book,* was published by Basfal Books (1994), and
the third, *Feeding the Fear of the Earth,* has been published
by Many Mountains Moving Press. The final installment
is *Breathe a Word of It,* the Air book, which is seeking a
publisher. The overall structure for the four books has
provided the author a vessel to pursue some innovative
approaches and an opportunity to explore recurring,
spiraling themes. The books fold into each other and
when combined create an alembic, an ensemble piece of
resonances with choreographic entanglements and aleatory
spillage. The collection is ecologically sensitive, creating a
network/netplay of emergent complexity and strange loops.

ABOUT THE AUTHOR

Patrick Lawler has published two earlier collections of poetry: *A Drowning Man is Never Tall Enough* (University of Georgia Press) and *reading a burning book* (Basfal Books). He has been awarded fellowships by the New York State Foundation for the Arts, the National Endowment for the Arts, and the Constance Saltonstall Foundation for the Arts. In addition to being an Associate Professor at SUNY College of Environmental Science and Forestry where he teaches Environmental Writing and Nature Literature, he teaches creative writing courses at Onondoga Community College. He is also part of the Creative Writing Program at LeMoyne College, where he teaches creative writing, playwriting, and writing for performance.

Visit the *Feeding the Fear of the Earth* web site
at www.mmminc.org